BREEDERS' BEST
A KENNEL CLUB BOOK™

Poodle

By Marcia A. Foy

BREEDERS' BEST
A KENNEL CLUB BOOK™

POODLE

ISBN: 1-59378-906-8

Copyright © 2004

Kennel Club Books, LLC
308 Main Street, Allenhurst, NJ 07711 USA
Printed in South Korea

10 9 8 7 6 5 4 3 2

PHOTOS BY:
Isabelle Français
and Bernd Brinkmann.

DRAWINGS BY:
Yolyanko el Habanero.

Contents

Meet the Poodle

T he Poodle is known in France as *le Caniche*, where he is considered to be the national dog, and in Germany as *der Pudel*, where he is considered to be a distinctly German creation. The Europeans, still arguing over who is the true originator of this ubiquitous and well-loved breed, divide the breed into four sizes. In the United States, where he is called the Poodle, he is known in three sizes, Toy, Miniature and Standard. No matter if he be small,

The Poodle, in all its sizes and colors, is one of the world's most intelligent, most recognizable and, of course, most popular breeds.

4

medium or large in size, this is an aristocratic, very intelligent dog who is likely the most flawless of canine companions. He is easy to train, loyal and reliable, not to mention glamorous, adaptable, courageous, agile and personable!

The Poodle is one of the oldest of all breeds of dog. It is difficult to trace the roots of nearly all dog breeds and, because of the Poodle's antiquity, it is even more difficult to trace his origins. Long before the French-German debate, Poodle-type dogs appeared on the tombs of the Greeks and Romans as early as 30 AD. In the 1400s, references to Poodles were seen in literature and in paintings. In fact, no other breed of dog has been pictured in art as often as the Poodle. Even the "Poodle trim," similar to the breed's hairstyles of today, were seen in these early paintings.

Some (Germans) would argue that the beginnings of the Poodle came

The Miniature Poodle embodies all of the wonderful Poodle traits in a conveniently small yet hardy size, making this an appealing variety for many a breed fancier.

Although the image of a glamorous, frilly, pampered pet often comes to mind when one thinks of the Poodle, the Standard variety is a large, strong dog, known for his athleticism and his ability as a protector of home and family.

first from Germany with probably some input into the breed from France and Russia. Others contend against that theory. In Germany, the translation of the breed's name, *Pudel,* is "to splash in the water," as the Poodle was used as a water retriever. In France, there were several types of Poodle. The Petit Barbet, which was a toy dog, probably descended from the Continental Toy Spaniel (Papillon) and the Maltese and the Caniche, which was a larger dog used for duck hunting. However, there was another dog in France, the only Poodle type that is a non-water dog, called the Truffle Dog. This dog worked the land, searching out the famous French truffles. Today, truffle-hunting dogs can still be found in Europe in the form of the Lagotta of Italy.

It was common practice to clip the profuse coat down so that the dog would be able to work in the water with greater ease. The hair was left on the head, chest and feet only, to protect those parts of the body from injury, and the hair was clipped from the rear to give the dog greater mobility in the water. The familiar Poodle clip of today has come down from this centuries-old custom.

Many photos of early Poodles depict dogs with corded coats, which were often seen in the Poodles of Germany, where the dogs had a more woolly coat texture and a tendency to cord. Eventually this coat texture died out, as it was difficult to keep in condition and not practical for everyday life. Nonetheless, corded Poodles can still be found today, though not commonly, and are acceptable in the show ring.

The three Poodle sizes in the US are the Standard Poodle, which is over 15 inches at the highest point of the shoulder; the Miniature Poodle, which is 15 inches and under; and the Toy Poodle, 10 inches and under at the shoulder (the Medium, recognized in Europe, is between the Standard and

Miniature). Other than size, all three Poodle varieties have the same breed standard and they are all considered to be the same breed, even though they an unprecedented run of popularity in the US, being the most popular of all breeds of dog from 1960 to 1983. At the present time, the Poodle

The Poodle as a water dog? Look into the breed's past and you'll find that this was one of the breed's original purposes. Many Poodles today take readily to the water, whether to retrieve or just to romp in the surf.

are shown in different groups at shows. The Toy, of course, is exhibited in the Toy Group, and the Miniature and Standard in the Non-Sporting Group.

Standard and Toy Poodles were shown in the United States prior to World War I. The Poodle's popularity continued to grow and, by the 1930s, the American public was becoming well aware of this delightful breed. By 1960, the Poodle had continues to rank in the top ten among breeds registered with the American Kennel Club (AKC).

The Poodle Club of America was founded in 1931 and immediately set to work developing a standard for breeders to follow. At that time, the Standard Poodle and the Miniature Poodle were considered as one variety. The Miniature Poodle, prior to the

1930s, had to compete with the Standard Poodle for Best of Breed to determine which would continue on to the Non-Sporting Group. The Toy Poodle was the second variety. It was not until 1943 that the Poodle Club of America recognized the Toys as the smallest variety of the breed and, after that, Toys could be bred down from Miniatures. The Toy variety improved in conformation, as well as adding a range of colors to the Poodle's coat. When the

In Germany, this dog's homeland, he is known as a *Kleinpudel*. This size is not recognized in the United States but is recognized in Europe as the Medium variety, falling in size between the Standard and Miniature varieties.

Miniature became the second variety of the Poodle, all three sizes were then able to enter their respective groups. The Standard Poodle and the Miniature Poodle both became able to represent their varieties in the Non-Sporting Group and the Toy Poodle represented his variety in the Toy Group.

Considered by most dog fanciers to be the show dog of show dogs, the Poodle excels in conformation competition like no other breed. Once bred to be a circus and performance dog, given the breed's high train-ability, intelligence and presence, the Poodle today makes a show dog *par excel-lence.* No other breed has acquired as many Best in Show awards as the Poodle. One cream-of-the-crop show dog is Ch. Whisperwind Is On A Carousel, a white Standard Poodle, who attained the outstanding record of 101 all-breed Bests in Show, including Best in Show at Westminster in 1991. The head of an exceptional line of winners, he was the sire of a multiple Best-in-Show winner, the grandsire of the Group winner at Westminster three years in a row and the great-grandsire of a dog who won the Group at Westminster in 2003.

The Poodle is certainly a dog to be considered when thinking of adding a pet to the household. He comes in three sizes, so you have a choice of a small, medium or large dog. In addition, you have a wide choice of colors from black and white to creams, apricots, browns, blues, grays and silvers! He is intelligent and relatively easy to train, and he will be a devoted companion for his lifetime.

Rowland Johns wrote in *Our Friend, The Poodle* in 1948: "There are no poker-faced specimens of this breed and they all have a wide facility for displaying, in their physiognomy, the signs that display the emotions by which human beings and dogs are so powerfully linked together."

MEET THE POODLE

Overview

- The Poodle is of European descent, with debate over whether his country of origin is France or Germany. The breed's antiquity makes his history hard to trace definitively.
- The Poodle's earliest utilization was as a water dog. Today's Poodle "hairstyles" derive from clips of old, designed to protect the dog and maximize his performance in the water.
- Three sizes of Poodle are recognized in the US, while four are recognized in Europe.
- The Poodle has enjoyed outstanding popularity in the US since its introduction into the country. He is a favored companion and consistently a top contender in the show ring.

Description of the Poodle

Every breed of dog registered with the American Kennel Club has a standard of perfection, which gives a mental picture of how the breed should look, act and move. The Standard Poodle and the Miniature Poodle are in the American Kennel Club's Non-Sporting Group. In general, Non-Sporting dogs are basically companion dogs. Other dogs in the Non-Sporting Group include the Bulldog, French Bulldog, Dalmatian and Boston Terrier. The Toy Poodle is, of course,

The most obvious characteristic of the Poodle is his coat, which is curly, dense and harsh in texture. It is seen in a variety of trims and a rainbow of colors and shades, among them the beautiful rich chocolate.

in the Toy Group, which includes the smallest of all of the breeds.

The first paragraph of the Poodle standard, under General Appearance, says it all: "That of a very active, intelligent and elegant appearing dog, squarely built, well proportioned, moving soundly and carrying himself proudly. Properly clipped in the traditional fashion and carefully groomed, the Poodle has about him an air of distinction and dignity peculiar to himself."

From the largest Standard to the smallest Toy, all Poodles are sturdily constructed dogs. The Standard Poodle is truly a powerhouse among canines.

He should have dark oval eyes with an intelligent expression, and his ear leathers are long and wide. His neck is long, and he carries his head high and with dignity. He has a deep chest and a short, broad, muscular loin. Note that this breed standard applies to all three varieties, so even though the Toy is very small, he looks identical to the Standard Poodle except in size.

His coat should be curly, though

The expression of the Poodle is intense and dignified, with intelligence glistening in the eyes. Black Poodles must have accompanying black pigmentation of the nose, eyerims and lips.

Occiput: Upper back part of skull; apex.

Skull: Cranium.

Stop: Indentation between the eyes at the point of nasal bones and skull.

Muzzle: Foreface or region of head in front of eyes.

Lips: Fleshy portion of upper and lower jaws.

Withers: Highest part of the back, at the base of neck above the shoulders.

Shoulder: Upper point of forequarters; the region of the two shoulder blades.

Forechest: Sternum.

Chest: Thoracic cavity (enclosed by ribs).

Forequarters: Front assembly from shoulder to feet.

Upper arm: Region between shoulder blade and forearm.

Elbow: Region where forearm and upper arm meet.

Forearm: Region between elbow and wrist.

Carpus: Wrist.

Brisket: Lower chest.

Pastern: Region between wrist (or heel) and toes.

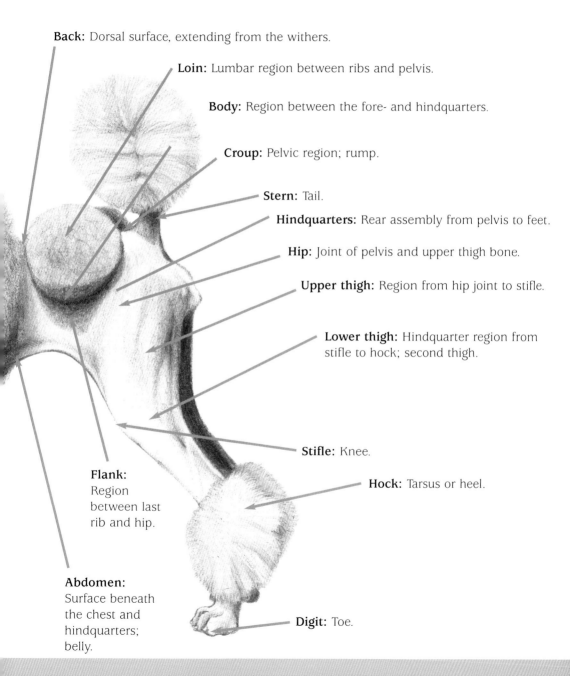

Back: Dorsal surface, extending from the withers.

Loin: Lumbar region between ribs and pelvis.

Body: Region between the fore- and hindquarters.

Croup: Pelvic region; rump.

Stern: Tail.

Hindquarters: Rear assembly from pelvis to feet.

Hip: Joint of pelvis and upper thigh bone.

Upper thigh: Region from hip joint to stifle.

Lower thigh: Hindquarter region from stifle to hock; second thigh.

Stifle: Knee.

Flank: Region between last rib and hip.

Hock: Tarsus or heel.

Abdomen: Surface beneath the chest and hindquarters; belly.

Digit: Toe.

naturally harsh with denseness throughout. The breed standard notes the following clips as being acceptable: a puppy clip for a Poodle under 12 months; the English saddle clip, whereby the face, throat, feet, forelegs and base of the tail are clipped; the Continental clip, with the legs having bracelets; and the sporting clip.

Unlike many other breeds, the Poodle comes in a wonderful variety of colors! He can be black, white, blue, gray, silver, brown, cafe-au-lait, apricot and cream, and the coat may show varying shades

The Continental clip features "anklets" on the dog's legs.

From silver to darker gray, a whole range of shades can be seen. A puppy's coat also can change in shade as he matures, deepening or lightening depending on the color.

of the same color. The nose color will vary with the color of the coat, meaning that dogs whose coats are shades of brown will have liver-colored noses, whereas the black, blue, gray, silver, cream and white Poodles will have black noses, eyerims and lips.

The gait of the Poodle should be proud, with the head held high. The standard notes: "A straightforward trot with light springy action and strong hindquarters drive. Head and tail carried up. Sound effortless movement is essential." He should have an air of dignity; shyness or sharpness is a major fault.

Do note that the Poodle, all three varieties, are pure-bred dogs that are registered with the American Kennel Club. Do not let a breeder tell you that his Peke-A-Poo, (Pekingese/Poodle cross) or his Cockapoo (Cocker Spaniel/Poodle cross) is a pure-bred dog. No matter how cute and sweet, these dogs will not be registered by the AKC and they will not

Some of the Poodle hairstyles feature elaborate topknots and sculptured grooming of the head. This Poodle possesses dark liver pigmentation to complement his apricot coat.

breed true to Poodle form. If you want a Poodle, look only for a pure-bred, AKC-registered Poodle.

DESCRIPTION OF THE POODLE

Overview

- The Standard and Miniature Poodle are classified in the AKC's Non-Sporting Group, while the Toy Poodle is a member of the Toy Group.
- Size is the only difference among the three Poodles; the same breed standard applies to all three sizes, with the size differences clearly stated.
- The breed standard emphasizes the Poodle's dignity in overall presence and expression.
- The coat receives much mention in the standard, as much attention is paid to the correct texture, acceptable clips and wide range of colors.

Are You a Poodle Person?

Poodle people are as distinctive a breed as the Poodle himself! Many a Poodle person grew up with Poodles, with Poodles being a part of the family life for generations. Other people are drawn to the Poodle because of his glamour and drama! Poodles are born entertainers, whether they are jumping through hoops, whirling around the show ring or just grinning pompon to pompon.

So, before you enter into the elite fraternity of Poodlephiles, you must give some thought to the personality

Nothing says glamour like a Poodle! Many dog lovers with a penchant for pet-pampering are attracted to the Poodle for just that reason.

and characteristics of this breed to determine if the Poodle is really the dog for you. This is not a pet for the laid-back owner who will not give the dog the training, the attention and the grooming that he deserves. This is a dog for the individual who is looking for an active, intelligent dog, a pet that will become a devoted companion and a true part of the family. He will want to be with you at all times and he will want to please you. Unlike dogs that can happily go their own way, the Poodle wants your attention! He is a bright dog that wants to please his owner. He is easy to train, will make an excellent watchdog and will be extremely loyal to the family.

Are you ready for an active, bright, personable companion to high-step his way into your heart and home?

You should answer the following questions before purchasing a Poodle:

1. Do you have the time to give to a dog? He will need care, companionship, training and grooming. throughout his entire lifetime.

Potential Poodle owners are certainly not lacking when it comes to choice. Size, color and how you will eventually clip your Poodle are some of the things to think about.

2. Do you have a fenced yard for your Poodle? He must have a secure area in which to run and exercise.

3. Have you owned a dog previously and did that dog live a long and happy life with your family?

4. Are you prepared to have a dog in your house that may weigh up to 75 pounds or weigh as little as 5 pounds? Each size has special needs.

5. Do you have time to groom your dog? In order to have a Poodle that looks like a Poodle, and because of the heavy coat, he will need at least a weekly grooming to avoid mats. If you are unable to clip and trim the Poodle yourself, will you have the time and money for a professional groomer?

Let's take each question one at a time:

1. Having time for a dog does not mean that you cannot work and own a dog. Your pet will need quality time, though. He must be fed on schedule and exercised several times a day. For the Standard Poodle, that means at least a long walk or a good romp in the morning and the evening. All Poodles need to be loved and will enjoy rides in the car with you. You must work with your Poodle to have an obedient dog with good manners.

2. A fenced yard will give your dog ample space. Never let him out loose to run the neighborhood. Remember, it is your responsibility to keep the yard clean of feces. When walking your dog, it is essential to carry a plastic bag or two to pick up droppings.

3. Previous dog ownership will give you a good idea of what a dog expects from you and what you must do for your dog. The Poodle is smart and needs an owner that is equally as smart as, or smarter than, he is!

4. The Standard Poodle is a large dog, not like a Miniature

or Toy Poodle who will sit on your lap. The Standard will take up a fair amount of space, whether on the sofa next to you or riding in the car. He will need ample room to run in his fenced-in yard, and he must have a crate that is large enough for him to be comfortable. The Toy Poodle, because of his tiny size, can be difficult to own if you have small children who like to roughhouse with a pet. The Miniature is average-sized and easy to fit into any household, although kids must still handle him with extreme care.

5. Grooming a heavily coated breed is nearly a constant job. The Standard, because he has more square inches to cover, requires the most time. If you do not groom regularly, your dog will become matted, dirty and smelly, and the grooming job will be considerable. Left long enough, you will have to take the dog to a groomer and have him shaved down. You want your dog to look like a Poodle, and a healthy one at that!

ARE YOU A POODLE PERSON?

Overview

- The Poodle is a special breed for a special breed of people! The rewards of Poodle ownership are many if you can devote the time and attention that the breed needs.
- The Poodle is extraordinary in many ways: beauty, intelligence, adaptability and athleticism in a loyal and loving companion.
- With the Poodle, you have three sizes from which to choose, promising the same delightful dog from large to small.
- Your lifestyle, living environment and family life will play deciding factors in which variety is best for you.

Selecting a Poodle Breeder

With a breed as popular as the Poodle, your selection of a breeder can be overwhelming. There are thousands of breeders in the US, dozens of whom are possibly in your city or county. Not every breeder is equal, nor is every Poodle puppy, no matter how precious and cute. Regardless of the variety of Poodle you wish to purchase, the breeder you select must be ethical and experienced. You want to buy a healthy puppy from a responsible breeder. A responsible breeder is someone who has given considerable

A good breeder will show you Mom right along with the pups. Assessing the dam's overall health and temperament gives you valuable insight into the quality behind the litter.

thought before breeding his bitch. He considers health problems in the breed, has room in his home or kennel for a litter of puppies and has the time to give to a litter. He does not breed to the dog down the block because it is easy and because he wants to have a litter to show his children the miracle of birth.

A responsible breeder is someone who is dedicated to the breed and to breeding out any faults and hereditary problems, and whose overall interest is in improving the breed. He will study pedigrees and see what the leading stud dogs are producing. To find the right stud dog for his bitch, he may fly his bitch across the country to breed to a particular stud dog, or he may drive the bitch to the dog, located a considerable distance away. He may have only one or two litters a year, which means that there may not be a puppy ready for you when you first call. Remember that

Take time when visiting the breeder to soak up as much about the breed as you can. Spend time with her and all of her Poodles, asking questions and learning from your interactions with the dogs.

The best kind of breeder raises and keeps her dogs in the home, not in a kennel environment. Of course, she is diligent about keeping the dogs' quarters in tip-top condition and will be happy to show you around.

CHAPTER 4

you are purchasing a new family member and usually the wait will be well worthwhile.

Check out the website *www.poodleclubofamerica.org* for a listing of local Poodle clubs. You should be able to find one in your area, or at least in your state, as there are many clubs. The local club should be able to refer you to responsible breeders and should be able to answer any questions that you may have.

The responsible Poodle breeder will probably be

You might not make it to Westminster like this cream-of-the-crop Poodle, but surely there are dog shows in your area at which you can observe dogs and make contacts within the breed.

someone who has been breeding for some years and someone who is known on the national level. He will be a member of the local Poodle

club and will likely belong to the Poodle Club of America. The responsible breeder will show you his kennel or invite you into his home to see the puppies. The areas will be clean and smell good. The breeder will show you the dam of the litter and she will be clean, smell good and be groomed. The puppies will also be clean, with toenails trimmed and clean faces. He may only show you one or two puppies, as he may choose not to show you the puppies that are already sold or that he is going to keep.

The breeder will have questions for you. Have you had a dog before? How many have you had and have you ever owned a Poodle? Did your dogs live long lives? Do you have a fenced yard? Do you intend to show or compete with your Poodle? How many children do you have and what are their ages? Are you willing to spend the time in teaching your children in how to treat the new family member? Have you ever done any dog training and are you willing to go to obedience classes with your dog? Are there any other pets in your household? Do not be offended by these and other questions. The breeder has put a lot of effort and money into his litter and his first priority is to place each pup in a caring and appropriate household where he will be wanted, loved and cared for. You should be more concerned if the breeder doesn't ask you any questions and is just quick to get your deposit. Never let a breeder rush you into the purchase of a puppy. Take your time and make the right decision.

Once you have passed his interrogation, you should ask the breeder some questions so that you are sure that he is an ideal breeder. Is he a member of the Poodle Club of America and a regional or local club? Does he show his own dogs or does he hire professional handlers? How many AKC champions has his kennel made? If the breeder

"doesn't have time for beauty pageants" or makes other derogatory statements about dog shows and the AKC in general, you should find another breeder. No established breeder has "made it" without conformation shows. The show

Without doubt, the breeder should be a true Poodle lover—and it should show!

ring is the proving ground for the whelping box. Only dogs who have proven that they are superior examples of the breed should be selected to create the next generation of Poodles.

Find out why he planned this breeding. Is the sire on the premises? If so, ask to meet the dog to assess his temperament, soundness and appearance. If he is not, ask to see other family members of the puppy. Likely the breeder has an aunt, half-sibling or cousin of the puppy that you could meet.

Review the pedigrees of the sire and dam. You should see titles on all of the grandsires and most of the granddams. "Ch.," "CDX" and "AAD" are indicators that these dogs excelled in the show ring, obedience trials and agility trials, respectively. Ask about health clearances for the sire and dam. The breeder should have documentation that his dogs have been screened for hip dysplasia with the Orthopedic Foundation for Animals (OFA) and for eye diseases with the Canine Eye Registration Foundation (CERF). Since the Poodle is prone to a number of hereditary conditions, breeders make a valiant effort never to breed affected dogs and have

Poodles love attention from their owners, and the feeling certainly is mutual. True Poodle devotees don't mind that their dogs are always underfoot (or under desk!).

The Orthopedic Foundation for Animals (OFA) was founded by John M. Olin and a group of caring veterinarians and dog breeders in the mid-1960s. The goal of the new foundation was to provide x-ray evaluations and guidance to dog breeders with regard to hip dysplasia, a common hereditary disease that affects many different breeds of dog.

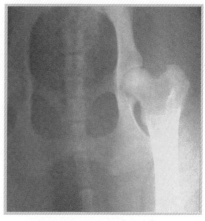

X-ray of a dog with "Good" hips.

Three board-certified OFA radiologists evaluate x-rays of dogs that are 24 months of age or older, scoring their hips as "Excellent," "Good" and "Fair," all of which are eligible for breeding. Dogs that score "Borderline," "Mild," "Moderate" and "Severe" are not eligible for breeding. The sire and dam of your new puppy should have OFA numbers, proving that they are eligible for breeding.

Since the OFA's inception, the organization has expanded to include databases on elbow dysplasia, patellar luxation, autoimmune thyroiditis, congenital heart disease, Legg-Calve-Perthes disease, sebaceous adenitis, congenital deafness, craniomandibular osteopathy, von Willebrand's disease, copper toxicosis, cystinuria, renal dysplasia and other diseases that have hereditary bases in dogs.

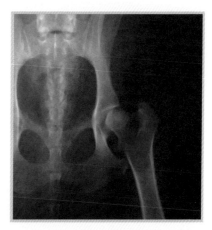

X-ray of a dog with "Moderate" dysplastic hips.

Visit the OFA website for more information on the organization, its history, its goals and the diseases from which it safeguards our pure-bred dogs. Go to www.offa.com.

If you want a Standard Poodle that will always be as athletic and animated as he should be, be sure to pick your pup from stock that has been tested and proven as free of hip dysplasia. Keep your Poodle prancing for his whole life!

relevant testing done. If the breeder claims that he doesn't screen for any hereditary conditions because "his dogs have never been affected," he may not be misleading you intentionally, but you should still not purchase from a breeder who does not have his dogs screened.

Find out also about the breeder's sales policy and review the sales agreement. You should expect to pay a signif-icant price for a well-bred Poodle puppy, but conscientious breeders guarantee their stock's health and soundness and will accept the puppy back with a refund or replacement if the dog develops a serious problem. Likewise, most breeders will accept a puppy back for up to a year if the match isn't right. In this case, however, you cannot expect a refund.

SELECTING A POODLE BREEDER

Overview

- Poodles, and thus Poodle breeders, can be found in droves. Finding a dedicated, ethical and reputable breeder will take more time and research, and this is the only source from which you should consider buying a puppy.
- Contact the AKC and the Poodle Club of America for referrals to trusted breeders.
- Prepare yourself beforehand with a list of questions for the breeder. When visiting, also be sure to look at the facilities, the litter, the parents and any other dogs on the premises.
- Remember that a good breeder will interrogate you, too!
- Ask to see all relevant documentation. Look for titles in the pup's pedigree, see appropriate health clearances and be sure that the breeder has a reasonable sales policy.

Finding the Right Puppy

What size is best for your family? The Standard Poodle is a hardy child's playmate, but caution must be taken with small children due to this variety's eventual large size, which could unintentionally overwhelm a child in play.

Before seeing the breeder and his pups, you should give some consideration as to whether you want to own a male or a female Poodle. Some individuals consider males easier to train but the more aggressive of the two sexes. Others prefer the softer disposition of a female. There are several factors that should be considered in making your decision. In general, the females will be somewhat smaller than the males. If you do not plan to neuter your pet (and some breeders will require you to neuter or spay your pet-only Poodle), a female will come into season approximately every six months. This can be a difficult time for up to three weeks, as it is fairly messy and hard on the house, and it will attract any "loose" males in the neighborhood, who will sit on your doorstep like lovelorn swains. Males who are not neutered can be more aggressive and will have more of a tendency to lift their legs and to mount your leg! If you are not sure which sex you want, discuss it with the breeder; he will be able to give you some direction.

Good pups come from good breeding. Before considering a litter, be sure to at least meet the mother and learn as much about the pups' pedigrees, ancestors and health backgrounds as possible.

With a breed as colorful as the Poodle, you probably have one or two color preferences in mind. If you have not set your heart on a color, good for you! Soundness of mind and body is far more important than the color of the pup's coat. The breed standard describes the vast rainbow of Poodle colors, but the only important consideration is

In a breed with such a variety of color choices, it's hard to pick a favorite! Nonetheless, esthetic points like color should be secondary to good health and sound temperament.

that the pup is solid-colored. Parti-colored Poodles are not too common these days, but there are still some breeders peddling "partis" as if they were better than the average Poodle. They are not, and they cannot be shown at AKC shows.

Now let's talk about the puppy's temperament. When looking over the pups, do not pick the puppy that hangs back

A pup's first socialization comes from his interactions with his "pack," namely his mom and littermates, as well as the breeder and the breeder's family.

and think twice before picking the extra-active, most outgoing of the litter. Hyper puppies can turn into hyper adults and will require more patience and time in training. Look for the middle-of-the-road puppy, the one that is interested, comes up to you, listens when you speak

and looks very alert. Never, but *never*, pick the pup that shies away and will not approach you. Never pick a puppy because you "feel sorry" for him. Don't forget that you are adding a new member to your family and you want one that is bright, healthy and, of course, fun!

The cost can be a factor when picking a large breed, such as the Standard Poodle. It is going to be much more expensive to feed a Standard Poodle than a Toy Poodle. In addition, the clean-up for the larger breed is much more extensive than for the small breed. If you have a breed that is tall, such as the Standard, you will need a higher fence and a larger yard. If you have the Toy Poodle, you can suffice with an exercise pen or a 3-foot-high fence. In addition, the crate for a large breed can run into a considerable amount of money. Small dog crates are less expensive. Once you have a dog, you realize that these are all factors that will play a part in your decision. But if you haven't owned a dog before, you are not aware of some of these "unseen" expenses.

PICKING FROM A PECK OF POODLE PUPS

You are now ready to select your Poodle puppy from a multi-colored peck of toddlers. You have decided that you are a Poodle person and that you can live with this inventive super-canine companion. Your entire family is ready for this new arrival into your home and lives. You have done your homework and have located a responsible breeder who has a litter available.

You arrive at the appointed time and the breeder has the puppies ready for you to look at. They should be a happy bunch, clean and groomed. Their noses will be wet, their coats will have a glow or sheen and they will have a nice covering of flesh over their ribs. You will be ready to pick up one of these rascals and cuddle him in your arms.

You should ask the breeder if the sire and dam of the litter have had their temperaments tested. These tests are offered by the American Temperament Test Society (ATTS) and responsible breeders will be familiar with this organization and will have had their animals tested. The breeder will show you the parents' score sheets, and you can easily determine if these are dogs with the personalities you are looking for. In addition, this is an excellent indication that this is a responsible breeder.

Temperament testing by the ATTS is done on dogs that are at least 18 months of age; therefore puppies are not tested, but the sire and dam of a litter can be tested. The test is like a simulated walk through a park or a neighborhood where everyday situations are encountered. Neutral, friendly and threatening situations are encountered to see what the dog's reactions are to the various stimuli. Problems that are looked for are unprovoked aggression, panic without recovery and strong avoidance. Behavior toward strangers, reaction to auditory, visual and tactile stimuli and self-protective and aggressive behavior are watched for. The dog is on a loose lead for the test, which takes about ten minutes to complete. On average, 80% of the Poodles tested passed the ATTS tests, which speaks well of the breed's sound temperament and stability.

Some breeders will have the temperaments of their puppies tested by a professional, their veterinarian or another dog breeder. By using these tests or through his own observations of the litter, the breeder will find the high-energy pup and the pup that will be slower in responding. He will find the pup with the independent spirit and the one that will want to follow the pack. If the litter has been tested, the breeder can suggest which pup he thinks will be best for your family. If the litter has not been tested, you can do a few simple tests while you are sitting on the floor, playing with the pups.

Pat your leg or snap your finger and see which pup comes up to you first. Clap your hands and see if any of the pups shy away from you. See how they play with one another. Watch for the one that has the most appealing personality to you, as this will probably be the puppy that you will take home. Look for the puppy that appears to be "in the middle," not overly rambunctious, overly aggressive or catatonic. You want the happy, cheerful pup, not the wild and crazy one. Spend some time selecting your puppy and, if you are hesitant, tell the breeder that you would like to go home and think over your decision. This is a major addition to the family, as you are adding a family member who may be with you for 10 to 15 years. Be sure you get the puppy that you will all be happy with.

ADOPTING AN ADULT

Aside from buying a puppy, there is another option for Poodle ownership: adopting a "rescue" Poodle. This will be a Poodle who, for a wide variety of reasons, is in need of a new home. This will usually be a dog over one year of age and very often is trained and house-broken. The breed rescue organization will bathe and groom the dog in addition to having a veterinarian's health certificate attesting to the good health of the dog. Usually these dogs make marvelous pets, as they are grateful for being in a loving home. Not only do the national clubs have an active rescue organization, but the local clubs will also have

How will you choose? With all of those sweet faces looking at you, it's easy to lose your heart, but a wise decision is only made by keeping your wits about you, taking your time and getting to know which pup suits you best.

groups of individuals working in this capacity. Rescue committees consist of very dedicated individuals who care deeply about the breed and give countless hours of their time, in addition to money, to assure that each dog will have a second chance at a happy home.

Do investigate the background of the rescue dog

A tiny pup is a huge responsibility, but with an equally huge reward if you choose carefully and raise him right.

Before your pup comes home, he may have had some exposure to a crate, such as during trips to the vet. This is advantageous, as it gives you a head start on crate-training.

as much as possible, as you do not want unforeseen problems to arise that someone else may have instilled in this particular dog. By going through the Poodle Club of America's rescue organization, you should be assured of getting a dog that you will be able to live with happily.

Another possibility is that the breeder may have an older dog that he wants to place in a good home. For some breeders, once they put a championship on a dog, they retire the dog to a pet home where he will receive the optimum of attention. Likewise, show dogs who were used in breeding programs may also be looking for good homes. Many breeders simply do not have the kennel space to house oodles of Poodles, so they need to find loving new homes for these great dogs. Do give this some thought, as often an older dog will be trained and easier to live with.

FINDING THE RIGHT PUPPY

Overview

- Male or female? Which color? Pet or show? After deciding on the Poodle variety, you have other factors to consider in making your puppy selection.
- Initial observations should reveal that all pups in the litter are healthy, clean and alert.
- Further observing the litter and taking the breeder's advice will guide you to a pup who is well suited to you temperamentally. The breeder may or may not have done formal temperament testing, but will have sufficient knowledge of each individual pup nonetheless.
- For those who wish to own a Poodle but would rather not raise a puppy, adoption of an adult Poodle from a breeder or rescue organization is a good option.

Welcoming the Poodle

What fun—the first day with your new Poodle in your home! Happy and exciting for you, but scary for your pup. First, let's make sure that you have everything you need before the puppy comes home. Certainly you wouldn't bring an infant home from the hospital without having a bed, a bottle, food, diapers, etc. Likewise, you have to be ready for your puppy's homecoming. Before welcoming your pup, you will need to purchase the basics, including puppy food, food and water pans and a leash and collar. The breeder will have recom-

Some Poodles like to stay on top of things, while others prefer to cozy up.

mended which food you should continue feeding your Poodle. A good pet shop will sell all of the items that you require, so go and take a leisurely stroll through the pet-supply store nearest you. There are plastic, ceramic, resin and stainless steel bowls, any of which will serve your purposes. Some owners prefer the stainless steel ones because they don't crack or chip and they can be sterilized. For a leash and collar, the nylon lightweight ones are the best, especially when working with a young Poodle.

The size of your bowl will depend on the size of your Poodle but, regardless of your dog's size, you want bowls that are sturdy, chew-proof and easy to clean.

You should also purchase a crate for your puppy, one that will accommodate him at his full size. The puppy not only will sleep in his crate but also will spend time there during the day when he is home alone. In very short order, your puppy

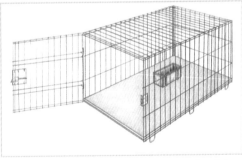

Meet your most valuable helper in your Poodle's training and safety: his crate. A wire crate is popular for use inside the home, as it gives your curious Poodle an unobstructed view of what's going on around him, making him feel part of his surroundings while safely confined.

will learn that the crate is his "second home" and he will feel safe and secure when he is in the crate. When the pup is left uncrated and alone, he will quickly become bored and begin to chew on the furniture, the corners of woodwork, whatever he can get his teeth on. Keeping him in a safe, confined area when you are

Where there's mischief to be made, that's where you'll find your puppy! Before your Poodle comes home, take a look at your house from a puppy's perspective and remove any potential for danger.

away can eliminate these problems. Be sure to add several towels or a washable blanket to the crate so that he will be comfortable.

Poodle owners love shopping for their pampered pets, but before you start accessorizing your Poodle with handcrafted jewelry and shiny bows, there are some other essentials for you to consider. To keep your Poodle looking glamorous, you are going to need to purchase some grooming supplies. A pin brush and a medium-toothed comb will help to keep the puppy coat clean and mat-free. Other items that you should consider are safe, durable toys (hard plastic bones, squeaky chase toys and nylon rope toys for chewing and play), a retractable leash (which come in various sizes and lengths, for long walks once the pup is trained to use a conventional lead), a pooper-scooper (for keeping your yard and neighborhood tidy) and a baby gate (for separating off-limits rooms).

If you are driving some distance to pick up your Poodle, take along a towel or two, a water pan and your leash and collar. Also take along some plastic baggies and a roll of paper towels in case there are any potty accidents or carsickness.

SAFETY AT HOME

Before bringing your puppy into the house, you should be aware that a small puppy can be like a toddler and there are dangers in the household that must be eliminated. Use common sense when raising a puppy and you should have few problems. Consider where a young child can get into trouble, and your puppy will be right behind him!

Electrical wires should be raised off the floor and hidden from view, as they are very tempting as chewable objects. Swimming pools can be very dangerous, so make certain that your puppy can't get into, or fall into, the pool. Some barricades will be necessary to prevent an accident. Poodles, with their water-dog background, should be excellent swimmers, but it is always wise to be cautious with young puppies and adults alike. Plus, your pool may be difficult for a dog to climb out of. Additionally, be careful about your deck or porch railings and make sure that your puppy cannot slip through the openings and fall.

Common sense, of course, is the owner's best defense, but Poodle owners also need to know some basic doggy facts to help keep their puppies safe:

- Dogs love chocolate, but

A puppy in the garden makes a cute picture, but it may not be safe for him to explore among the flowers if there are poisonous plants, fertilizers or other hazards present.

chocolate kills dogs. Any kind of candy, cookie or dessert that contains chocolate or cocoa is toxic to dogs.
- Fertilizers and other lawn treatments are harmful to dogs. Be especially wary of rose fertilizers, which can kill a pup or grown dog. Mulch that contains cocoa hulls can also be harmful to dogs.
- Antifreeze, like chocolate, is sweet and toxic to dogs. Keep it out of reach or in the trunk

Poodles are bright and investigative dogs, so it's best to keep them occupied rather than allowing them to create their own diversions. Safe, durable dog toys will keep your dog's mind away from exploring himself right into trouble!

of your car, somewhere where your dog can't get to it.

- Paints, paint thinner, varnishes, etc., can harm your dog. Never spray-paint your Poodle. Groomers may be able to help you color your Poodle for a special occasion (like a family wedding or the Fourth of July), but never attempt to do it with a household spray paint. Don't laugh—it's been done.

If you have young children in the house, you must see that they understand that the small puppy is a living being and must be treated gently. They cannot roughhouse with him, pull his ears or pick him up and drop him. This is your responsibility. A child taught about animals at an early age can become a lifelong compassionate animal lover and owner.

SETTLING IN
When puppy comes into the house for the first time (after he

Just as important as buying the puppy accessories, you must 'puppy-proof' your house. Poodle pups are naturally curious critters that will investigate everything new, then seek-and-destroy just because it's fun. The message here is: never let your puppy roam your house unsupervised. Scout your house for the following hazards:

Trash Cans and Diaper Pails
These are natural puppy magnets (they know where the good smelly stuff is!)

Medication Bottles, Cleaning Materials, Roach and Rodent Poisons
Lock these up. You'll be amazed at what a determined puppy can find.

Electrical Cords
Unplug wherever you can and make the others inaccessible. Injuries from chewed electrical cords are extremely common in young dogs.

Dental Floss, Yarn, Needles and Thread, and Other Stringy Stuff
Puppies snuffling about at ground level will find and ingest the tiniest of objects and will end up in surgery. Most vets can tell you stories about the stuff they've surgically removed from puppies' guts

Toilet Bowl Cleaners
If you have them, throw them out now. All dogs are born with 'toilet sonar' and quickly discover that the water there is always cold.

Garage
Beware of antifreeze! It is extremely toxic and even a few drops will kill an adult Poodle, less for a pup. Lock it and all other chemicals well out of reach. Fertilizers can also be toxic to dogs.

Socks and Underwear, Shoes and Slippers, Too
Keep them off the floor and close your closet doors. Puppies love all of the above because they smell like you times ten!

CHAPTER 6

Your Poodle's sleeping habits, including a regular sleeping place and bedtime set forth from puppyhood, help to reinforce the daily routine throughout his life. Of course, when he's ready to start his day, you may get a wake-up call!

has relieved himself outside), let him look at his new home and surroundings, and give him a light meal and a pan of water. When he is tired, take him outside again for another potty trip and then tuck him into his crate, either to take a nap or, hopefully, to sleep through the night.

The first day or two for your puppy should be fairly quiet. He will then have time to get used to his new home, surroundings and family members. The first night, he may cry a bit, but if you put a teddy bear or a soft, woolly sweater in his crate, this will give him some warmth and security. A nearby ticking clock or a radio playing soft music can also be helpful. Remember, he has been uprooted from a sibling or two, his mother and his familiar breeder, and he will need a day or two to get used to his new family. If he should cry this first night, let him be and he will eventually quiet down and sleep. By the third night, he should be well settled in. Have patience and, within a week or less, it will seem to you, your family and puppy that you have all been together for years.

WELCOMING THE POODLE

Overview

- Before your pup comes home, you must have all of the necessary puppy supplies on hand.
- Equally as important as your puppy shopping spree is creating a safe "puppy-proof" environment indoors and outdoors.
- Your puppy is making a big transition from the breeder's home to yours, so you must help him feel comfortable and settle in.
- Take it slow during the first few days, as your pup is getting adjusted. Make family introductions low-key, being especially careful with children, and give him constant supervision to ensure his safety.

Your Poodle's First Lessons

L et's begin the puppy's education with two basic but vital lessons. We are going to teach the puppy to come to his owner when called and to accept a collar and leash. The "come" lesson can be reinforced by playing games with your puppy. Games are a great way to entertain your puppy and yourself, while subliminally teaching lessons in the course of having fun. Start with a game plan and a pocketful of tasty dog treats. Keep your games short so you don't push his attention

The come command can begin as a game, coaxing your Poodle to come to you for a toy and then throwing it for him to fetch and bring back.

span beyond normal puppy limits.

The "puppy catch-me" game is ideal to teach the puppy recall. With two people sitting on the floor about 10 or 15 feet apart, one person holds and pets the pup while the other calls him: "Prince, come!" in a happy voice. When the pup comes running, lavish big hugs on him and give him a tasty treat. Repeat back and forth several times, maybe adding a ball for the puppy to retrieve.

A buckle collar is the best choice for both pup and adult, as it is comfortable for the dog to wear and can be adjusted easily as needed.

Another fun game that teaches the come lesson is hide and seek. Play this game outdoors in your yard or some other confined area. When the pup is distracted, hide behind a tree, a bush or other large object. Peek out to see when he realizes that you are gone and comes running back to find you. As soon as he gets close, come out, squat down with arms outstretched and call him: "Prince, come!" This is a good technique and teaches the pup to depend on you.

Once your Poodle is accustomed to walking on lead, he can graduate to a retractable lead for your daily walks. Your dog will appreciate the freedom of a wider area to explore, while you will appreciate that the lead retracts when you want to keep him close to you.

To introduce your puppy to the leash and collar, rely on your positive training techniques. You have purchased a nice new nylon collar and leash and you're going to show them to the puppy. He's not going to be all that thrilled to meet his first of many restraining devices, but let's pretend this is fun for him. "Look, Prince. A collar! Good collar. See, good boy, good leash!" Puppies are impressionable, so surely Prince's pompon is wagging by now. With no further fanfare, put the collar on the pup with the leash attached and walk away. Many a pup will panic and try to remove the collar (he can't) and soon enough he'll stop squealing.

Now begin to play one of your games. Hide and seek works well here. You can also just have the puppy follow you around for a treat. After ten minutes, remove the collar and leash, and repeat the routine tomorrow. By the third day of the puppy's following you around, you are ready to "take the lead." Now let the puppy lead you around the house or the yard. The leash is no reason to be afraid, so don't start scaring Prince by tugging him around the block.

By the fourth or fifth day, you can take the lead and start asserting your leadership role. Lead him around gently, without tugging. This is not his first heeling lesson, just an introduction to his new nylon friends. We'll teach him to heel in a couple of weeks.

GOOD FIRST IMPRESSIONS
Poodles are people dogs. They thrive on interaction with humans, even more so than they crave the company of the other dogs. Turning your Poodle into the most popular socialite on your block will not take too much effort on your part. Your Poodle has pizzazz, oomph and chutzpah!

The puppy's dam and breeder start the socialization

process at the kennel. Now it's your turn to take the lead and show your Poodle to the world. Socializing your puppy is very important if you want a dog that fits into the human world and that is a good companion who is enjoyed by everyone.

Socializing a puppy is similar to when you bring home a new baby. Hold and pet your puppy so that he knows that he is wanted and loved. Do not play with him constantly, though, as he is very young and needs time to rest up and sleep. Keep him to a schedule as much as you can, as he will become schedule-oriented very quickly. If he knows that you rise at 7 a.m. every day, and shortly after you will take him out, he will wait for you to let him out before relieving himself in his crate.

Habits, and that includes good and bad habits, that are learned at an early age become lifelong habits, so it is best to start out on the right foot. Don't let him chew on an old shoe or

sock and think that it's cute, because before long he will chew on your Versace loafers and cashmere socks. (Poodles have taste, you know.) Lay out the rules and stick to them: do not eat Daddy's clothes (no matter how terrific they smell!).

Out and about the pampered Poodle way! Many owners of smaller-variety Poodles truly love to "baby" their dogs.

Keep the pup confined to a specific area, such as the kitchen or den, until he is trained and fairly mature. Use baby gates and he will quickly learn that he is welcome in certain areas of the house and not welcome in other areas. And, of course, put him into his crate when you leave home. He will be comfortable in his "house" and he will sleep until you come home.

NOM DE POODLE

One of the important factors in training a young pup is to give him a name. Sometimes it may take a week or so before you find a name that fits the dog. Other times, you will have him named before you bring the

Socialization with children of all ages will help your Poodle become well adjusted to everyone he meets. It goes without saying that an adult must be present to supervise all dog-child introductions and interactions.

puppy into the house. Don't forget the Poodle's French (and/or German and/or Russian origins) when you name your dog. Choose a name that befits the breed's heritage and nationality.

The name on your dog's pedigree will not be his call name. The dog's official AKC name will incorporate the breeding kennel's prefix (like Braylane, House Yoko or Dawin) with a clever phrase. Call names are just that, what you use to call your dog. In general, short one- or two-syllable call names are the easiest for training, such as "No, Fifi." It becomes more difficult when you have to say, "No, Remy Martin" or "Sit, Napoleon." You do, however, get points for trying to name your dog after expensive brandies and desserts!

You want a name that not only fits the personality of the dog but your own personality as well. You're the one who has to say it 400 times a day. If you're not going to be comfortable bellowing "Stella!" into your back yard (and who are you anyway, Marlon Brando?), then pick one that you're happy with. Some popular choices are Jacques,

Beau, Belle and Jean (if you're on the French side of the fence). If you have a white Poodle, you can name her Blanche; then, when it's kibbletime, you can say, "Eat your din-din, Blanche!" Poodles don't like German names because they're too harsh-sounding for this elegant breed. You never hear a handler in the ring say, "Heel, Hans, Heel!" Choose a snappy French name and your dog will quickly know that you are talking about him. Of course, you will be expected to use the correct French pronunciation!

CAR RIDES

You should get your dog used to riding in the car at an early age. Teach him some car manners, such as not riding on the driver's lap, no racing about the car from window to window and no chewing on the arm rests. In his crate is the safest way for him to travel. Do not take your dog out on a hot day and leave him alone for even a few minutes in the car. A car can heat up very quickly in the summer months, and the dog will not be able to cope with the heat.

YOUR POODLE'S FIRST LESSONS

Overview

- The come command is one of the most important lessons that your Poodle will learn, and you can start teaching him early on in the form of fun games with you.
- Socializing your Poodle will be easy; he's a true people magnet! Exposing him to different people, animals and situations as a pup will help him to grow up well adjusted and confident.
- Encourage your pup's good behavior and good habits by keeping him out of trouble. In a safe confined area, with all temptation out of reach, he has no choice but to be a "good boy."

House-training Your Poodle

L et's face it: it's no fun mopping up Poodle puddles! Housebreaking makes the difference between a nice, neat home where the owner and dog live together in harmony and a smelly, untidy home where the owner is frustrated by his dog's excretory habits. So let's start by saying that your dog must be house-broken and this job should begin as soon as you bring him home. Diligence during the first two or three weeks will surely pay off. As a Poodle owner you are lucky, because this should be a relatively easy job with such a smart and trainable dog.

Clean living with your Poodle starts with training him to use the outdoors for his relief needs.

Every time your puppy wakes up from a nap, he should be quickly taken outside. Watch him and praise him with "Good boy!" when he urinates or defecates. Give him a pat on the head and take him inside. He may have a few accidents but, with the appropriate "No" from you, he will quickly learn that it is better to go outside and do his "job" than to do it on the kitchen floor and be scolded. When cleaning up after you dog, use a safe deodorizer and really clean the floor. Dogs can smell where they soiled and return there again and again.

A travel crate is a wonderful safety tool for car rides and trips, but the crate your Poodle uses as his "den" in your home should be a bit roomier and preferably made of wire so that he won't feel boxed in.

You will soon learn the habits of your dog. However, at the following times it is essential to take your dog out: when he gets up in the morning, after he eats, before he goes to bed and after long naps. As he matures, most dogs will have to go out only three or four times a day. Some dogs will go to the door and bark when

Lifting a leg is more than just a bathroom behavior; in males, it's a "calling card" of sorts to let other dogs know that they stopped by the rose bush, fire hydrant, telephone pole, etc.

they want to be let out and others will nervously circle around. Watch and learn from your Poodle's signs.

THE CRATE ADVANTAGE

You have already been advised to purchase a crate for your puppy. This will be your favorite piece of equipment, because it's a major house-breakthrough! Crate training, hands and paws down, is the most efficient way to house-train a pup. Accustom the puppy to the crate on his first day in your home. Since dogs instinctively want to keep their crates tidy, they will not soil their crates. This theory goes back to the ancient canine's life in a den. Dogs do not mess where they eat or sleep. It's actually that simple.

What complicates crate training is also simple: you! Inexperienced (and/or stubborn) dog owners associate the crate not with a dog's den but with the federal penitentiary or a furrier's trapping device! "I can't lock my little Josephine up!" "It's so cruel to see my dog trapped in that little cage." Dogs don't hate crates, owners do. Give your Poodle pup a day or two to adjust and you will save both of you years of frustration.

If you purchased your Poodle from an experienced breeder, you may already have "the crate advantage." Many breeders introduce the litters to crates before the pups even leave for their new homes. This saves the new owner an important step. The sense of security and structure that the crate provides proves valuable in so many ways. Dogs respond to crate training and choose to spend time in their crates during the day and will sleep the whole night through in their crates with nary a peep.

Always be patient with housebreaking, as this can sometimes be a trying time.

Crates don't promise miracles, because we are still dealing with the immature body and mind of a puppy. With common sense and consistency, you will soon have a clean house dog. Soon your life will be much easier for all of you—not to mention better for the carpeting!

Keep in mind while training: use your common sense, be consistent and have patience. Just when you may think that all is hopeless, your puppy turns into the perfect little gentleman who never soils his home or yours!

If you don't have a yard to accommodate your Poodle's needs, you will have to take him out for potty breaks. Of course, you will be a responsible dog owner and bring all you need to clean up after him.

HOUSE-TRAINING YOUR POODLE

Overview

- It is necessary to begin housebreaking, teaching proper toileting habits, right away when your puppy comes home.
- Your speed and success in housebreaking depends largely on your consistency and diligence in sticking to a schedule.
- Crate training is recognized by many as the most effective way to housebreak a dog. Learn how to use a crate properly.
- Know the times at which it is necessary to bring your Poodle outdoors; at other times, learn to recognize the signs that he needs to go out.

School Days for the Poodle

Isn't that the face of a straight-A student? Poodles are enjoyable to train because they are quick to learn and capable of so much.

If you have acquired your Poodle puppy from a responsible breeder, the pup should be on the way to being well socialized when you bring him home. He will be used to family and strangers, and average noises in the house and on the street will not startle him. Socialization for your puppy is very important, and most breeders begin early socialization with their litters. It is especially helpful if there are children in the family. Once your're in your home, let your pup meet the neighbors and let him play a few minutes. Take him for short walks in public places where he will see people and other dogs as well as hear strange noises. Watch other dogs, however, as they are not always friendly. Keep your dog on a short leash and you will have control over him so he does not jump on anyone.

You will find it to your advantage to have a mannerly dog; therefore some basic commands will make your dog a better canine citizen. One of the family members should attend Puppy Kindergarten classes, from which all further training will grow. This is a class that accepts puppies from two to five months of age and takes about two months to complete. You will cover the basics: sit, heel, down, stay and recall (or come). There are definite advantages to each. The sit and heel exercises are great helps when walking your dog. Who needs a puppy walking between your legs, lunging forward or lagging behind, in general acting unruly?

Incorporate play in between your training sessions to make lesson time fun and to keep your Poodle's interest and enthusiasm high.

You and your Poodle will enjoy a fulfilling dog/owner bond if you take the time to understand each other's language.

You want to have your dog walking like a gentleman on your left side and sitting as you wait to cross the street. Recall is very important if your dog escapes from the yard, breaks his leash or otherwise gets away from you and you need to call him back. Remember, it is essential to have an obedient pet.

Here is a short rundown of the commands. If you attend puppy classes or obedience training classes, you will have

How you approach training will differ somewhat according to your variety of Poodle. With the smaller varieties, it is advisable to crouch down so as not to intimidate.

professional help in learning these commands. However, you and your dog can learn these very basic exercises on your own.

SIT

This is the first exercise with which you should begin. Place your dog on your left side as you are standing and firmly say "Sit." As you say this, run your hand down your dog's back and gently push him into a sitting position. Praise him, hold him in this position for a few minutes, release your hand, praise him again and give him a treat. Repeat this several times a day, perhaps as many as ten times, and before long your pup will understand what you expect of him.

STAY

Teach your dog to stay in a seated position until you call him. Have your dog sit and, as you say "Stay," place your hand in front of his nose and take a step or two, no more at the beginning, away from him. After ten seconds or so, call your dog. If he gets up before the end of the command, have him sit again and repeat the stay command. When he stays until called (remembering to start with a very short period of time), praise him and give him a treat. As he learns this command, increase the space that you move away from the dog as well as the length of time that he stays.

A gentle push on the rump will guide your Poodle into the correct sit position. Once he knows what is expected of him, learning (and teaching) the sit is a snap!

HEEL

Have your dog on your left side, with his leash on, and teach him to walk with you. If your pup lunges forward, give the leash a quick snap and say a firm "No." Then continue to walk your dog, praising him as he walks nicely by your side. Again, if he lunges, snap his leash quickly and say a smart "No." He will quickly learn that it is easier and more pleasant to

Your outstretched arm with your palm facing the dog acts as a "stop sign," indicating along with your verbal command that the dog should stay put until you give the OK.

walk by your side. Never allow him to lunge at someone passing by you.

COME

Always practice this command on leash. You can't afford to risk failure, or your pup will learn that he does not have to come when called. Once you have the pup's attention, call him from a short distance with "Puppy, Come!" (use your happy voice!) and give a treat when he comes to you. If he hesitates, tug him to you gently with his leash. Grasp and hold his collar with one hand as you dispense the treat. This is important. You will eventually phase out the treat and switch to hands-on praise. This maneuver also connects holding his collar with coming and treating, which will assist you in countless future behaviors. Do 10 or 12 repetitions 2 or 3 times a day. Once pup has mastered the come command, continue to

The sit/stay exercise begins with you and the dog side by side, with the dog in the sit position. Be sure to have his attention focused on you before you step out in front of him to begin the stay.

A dog with proper on-lead manners is a must! Regardless of your Poodle's size, your daily walks will be quite a hassle if you have to deal with a dog who pulls ahead, lags behind or otherwise refuses to walk with you politely.

Use a treat or a favorite toy to coax your Poodle into the down position.

practice daily to engrave this most important behavior into his brain. Experienced Poodle owners know, however, that you can never completely trust a dog to come when called if the dog is bent on a self-appointed mission. "Off leash" is often synonymous with "out of control."

DOWN

This will probably be the most complicated of the five basic commands to teach. Place your dog in the sit position, kneel down next to him and place your right hand under his front legs and your left hand on his shoulders. As you say "Down," gently push the front legs out into the down position. Once you have him down, talk gently to him, stroke his back so that he will be comfortable and then praise him.

MORE EVERYDAY COMMANDS

There are some commands that are not taught in obedience class that you and

In teaching commands, you can use hand signals along with your verbal commands as long as you are consistent with both.

your dog will learn on your own. "Off" is an important command, especially with a Standard Poodle, as he will become tall enough to finish off the candy dish on the coffee table or reach onto the kitchen table for the butter. Tell him "Off, Jacques" and then push him down on his four feet. This command also comes in handy if your Poodle jumps up on people or forbidden furniture. Again, dogs are smart, particu-

For potential show dogs, it is necessary to teach the stay in the standing position, as they will be required to stand in the ring for the judge's evaluation.

larly Poodles, and he will quickly learn what "Off" means.

Another good command is "Kennel up," telling the dog to go to his crate. Along with "Kennel up" you should teach "Bedtime!" and this will also tell him to go to his crate. Do not confuse the two, however, and tell him "Bedtime" when you are only going to the store and will be back in an hour. Your

Your intelligent Poodle is a natural performer and capable of learning many charming tricks, like "dancing" on hind legs for a treat.

Conformation showing brings your training and communication to the next level. Poodles are popular show dogs, and it's easy to see why! They look sensational and create quite a lot of excitement in the ring.

Poodle will quickly learn that "Bedtime" means a treat and to bed for the night. "Kennel up" means that you will be back in

a little while. And, of course, the most basic of commands, which is learned very quickly, is "No." Say it firmly and with conviction. Again, your dog will learn that this means to keep off, don't do it or don't even think about it.

In all of your commands, you must be fair (don't tell him

to sit when he is already sitting), you must be consistent (don't let him jump onto the sofa sometimes and not at other times) and you must be firm in delivering every command (like "No, Jean Pierre"). After the dog does what you want, give him a pat on the head and praise: "Good dog, Jean Pierre." If he has achieved some great success, give him a treat along with the praise.

Big parts of training are patience, persistence and routine. Teach each command the same way every time, do not lose your patience with the dog, as he will not understand what you are doing, and reward him for performing his command properly. With a Poodle, you will find that your puppy will learn these commands very quickly and you will be thrilled with your dog's good manners. Your friends, when they come to your house for a dinner party, will also appreciate a well-behaved dog who will not jump on their clothing or land in their laps while they are having cocktails.

SCHOOL DAYS FOR THE POODLE

Overview

- Before formal training begins, your puppy will be on the road to good behavior if he is well socialized.
- Basic commands like sit, stay, come, heel and down are the building blocks to a well-behaved, reliable Poodle.
- Knowledge of commands is necessary for your dog's safety as well as his good behavior.
- Other helpful commands include "Off," "No" and instructions to let your dog know that it's time to go to his crate.
- Keep your Poodle well versed in the commands by incorporating them into your daily routine whenever possible.

Home Care for Your Poodle

Once your Poodle is mature and remaining well, he will only need a yearly visit to the veterinary clinic for a check-up and a booster shot for his vaccines. A dental exam should be part of these visits, and you may also want to have the vet check your dog's anal glands.

For home dental care, you may purchase a dental tool and clean the teeth yourself. Set the dog on the grooming table, with his head in the noose, and gently scrape away any tartar. Some animals will let you do this and others will not, but may accept a soft toothbrush with

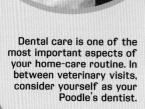

Dental care is one of the most important aspects of your home-care routine. In between veterinary visits, consider yourself as your Poodle's dentist.

special toothpaste for dogs. A dog treat every night before bedtime will also help to keep the tartar down.

As for the anal glands, expressing them is not the most pleasant of tasks, besides being quite smelly. You may find that it is easier to have this done during the yearly trip to the vet. On occasion the anal glands will become impacted, requiring veterinary attention to clean them out.

Ear problems, like mites or infections, require medicated ear drops to eradicate. Owners must be consistent in administering the medication for the full course of treatment.

FIRST AID

Every home with a pet should have a first-aid kit. You can acquire all of these items at one time to have on hand, kept in a box to be easily accessible. Here are the items you will need:

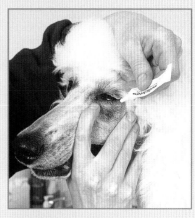

An ointment or salve may be prescribed for certain eye problems. Light-colored Poodles also may be prone to tear stains, which can be removed with a special cleansing product.

- Alcohol for cleaning a wound;
- Antibiotic salve for treating the wound;
- Over-the-counter eye wash in case your dog gets something in his eyes or just "to get the red out";

- Forceps for pulling out wood ticks, thorns and burs;
- Styptic powder for when a toenail has been trimmed too short and bleeds;
- Rectal thermometer;
- A nylon stocking to be used as a muzzle if your pet should be badly injured.

WELLNESS OF YOUR DOG

By now, you know your dog well, you know how much he eats and sleeps and how hard he plays. As with all of us, on occasion he may "go off his feed" or appear to be sick. If he has been nauseated for 24 to 36 hours, or had diarrhea for the same amount of time, or has drunk excessive water for five or six days, a trip to the veterinarian is in order. Make your appointment and tell the receptionist why you need the appointment now.

The veterinarian will ask you the following questions:
- When did he last eat a normal meal?
- How long has he had diarrhea or been vomiting?
- Has he eaten anything in the last 24 hours?
- Could he have eaten a toy or a piece of clothing or anything else unusual?
- Is he drinking more water than usual?

The vet will check him over, take his temperature and pulse, listen to his heart, feel his stomach for any lumps, look at his gums and teeth for color and check his eyes and ears. He will probably also draw blood to run tests.

At the end of the examination, the vet will diagnose your dog's problem and decide how to treat it. He may send your dog home with you with some antibiotics, take some x-rays or keep the dog overnight for observation. Follow your vet's instructions and you will find that very often your dog will be back to normal in a day or two. In the meantime, feed him light meals and keep him quiet, perhaps confined to his crate.

BUGS AND OTHER NUISANCES

Parasites can be a problem, and there are certain ones of which you should be aware. Heartworm can be a deadly problem; some parts of the country can be more prone to this than others. Heartworms become very massive and wrap themselves around the dog's heart. If not treated, the dog will eventually die.

In the spring, call your veterinarian and ask if your dog should have a heartworm test. If so, take him to the clinic, where he will be given a test to make certain that he is clear of heartworm and then he will be put on a heartworm preventative. Most puppies are tested and started on a preventative program early in life. This is important, particularly if you live near water where mosquitoes like to breed.

Fleas are also a problem, but particularly in the warmer parts of the country. You can purchase flea powder or a collar from the pet shop or ask your veterinarian what he suggests that you use. There are many effective spot-on

You never know what might be lurking in the grass, sizing up your Poodle's coat as a suitable home.

treatments that combat fleas, ticks and other pests. If you suspect fleas, lay your dog on his side, separate the coat to the skin and see if you see any skipping, jumping or skittering around of little bugs.

Ticks are more prevalent in wooded or grassy areas. Ticks are small (to start) and dark, and like to attach themselves to the warm parts of the ear, the leg pits, face folds, etc. The longer they stay on the dog, the bigger they become, filling themselves with your pet's blood and becoming as big as a dime. Take your forceps and carefully pull the tick out to make sure you get the pincers. Promptly flush the tick down the toilet or light a match to it. Put alcohol on the wound and a dab of antibiotic salve.

Let common sense and a good veterinarian be your guide in coping with all canine health issues.

SENIOR POODLES

As your dog starts aging, he will start to slow down. He will not play as hard or as long as he used to and he will sleep more. He will find the sunbeam in the morning hours and take a long nap. At this time, you will probably put him on a senior dog food, but do continue to watch his weight. It is more important than ever not to let your senior citizen become obese. You will notice that his muzzle will become gray and you may see opacities in his eyes, signs of cataracts. As he becomes older, he may also become arthritic.

Continue your walks, making them shorter, and give him a baby aspirin when he appears to be stiff. Keep the grooming up, as both you and he will like to have him looking and smelling good. Watch for lumps and bumps and take him to the veterinarian if you notice any abnormalities. Incontinence can also become a problem with the older dog. While this is frustrating for you and hard on the house, he hasn't become "unhousebroken"; rather, his excretory muscle

Caring for your Poodle includes providing him with proper identification. Tattooing is a popular form of permanent ID, and the light-colored skin of the ear flap makes the tattoo easily visible.

control is fading.

Veterinary care has changed much over the last decade or two, as has medical care for humans. Your veterinarian can now do much to extend your dog's life if you want to spend the money. While this will extend his life, it will not bring back his youth. Your primary concern should be to help your Poodle live out his life comfortably, and there are medications that can be helpful for him. Whatever you do, try to put your dog and his well-being and comfort ahead of your emotions and do what will be best for your pet.

Always remember the many wonderful years that your Poodle gave to you and your family and, with that thought, it may not be long before you are looking for a new puppy for the household. And there you are, back at the beginning with a cute bundle of joy, ready for another ten years or more of happiness!

HOME CARE FOR YOUR POODLE

Overview

- In between veterinary visits, your dog's health care is in your hands.
- Have a well-stocked canine first-aid kit as well as basic knowledge of emergency-care techniques.
- Know your dog well so you can recognize the signs when something is wrong.
- Safe and effective parasite control is a must; discuss preventative options with your vet.
- An older dog requires more attention to his care, a small price to pay for the years of happiness he's given you.

Feeding Your Poodle

N utrition for your puppy is actually very easy. Dog-food companies hire many scientists and spend millions of dollars on research to determine what will be a healthy diet for your dog. Your breeder should have been feeding a premium puppy chow and you should continue on with the same brand. Your young puppy will probably be fed three times a day, perhaps as many as four times a day. As he matures, you will reduce his meals to two times a day, dividing his daily portion into morning and evening feedings.

The breeder starts the litter off on a good-quality solid food after they are weaned from their mother. Take the breeder's advice about how best to feed your new puppy once he comes home and how to change his diet as he matures.

When your Poodle reaches eight months of age, you will change over to the adult formula of the same type of dog food. Do not add vitamins or anything else unless your veterinarian suggests that you do so. You can check your dog-food bag for the amount, per pound of weight, that you should be feeding your dog. To the dry kibble, you can add water to moisten and possibly a tablespoon or so of a canned dog food for flavor. It's that simple. Do not think that by cooking up a special diet you will turn out a product that will be more nutritional than what the dog-food companies are providing.

Standard Poodle owners may consider elevated stands on which to place their dogs' food and water bowls. There is some debate, however, about whether this feeding method is helpful or detrimental; discuss this with your vet.

Keep the table treats to a minimum, remembering that some "people foods" (like chocolate, onions, nuts, grapes, raisins) are toxic to dogs, and give him a dog treat at bedtime. Keep a good covering of flesh over his ribs, but do not let your dog become a fat boy! However, the

"What do you have for me?" No dog can ignore the call of his dinner bowl, and your Poodle will pop up out of nowhere when there's food to be had!

CHAPTER 11

more active the dog, the more calories he will need. And always have fresh drinking water available. This may include a pan of water in the kitchen and another outside for time spent in the yard.

When feeding a Poodle, quality—not quantity—must be stressed. Select the top-quality brand to feed your Poodle, relying on the advice of your breeder and/or veterinarian. Surely, the better foods cost more, but the higher priced products pay off when feeding your dog. As many experienced breeders say, "First you breed a coat and then you feed a coat." With a coated breed like the Poodle, who has the most magnificent coat in dogdom, an owner has to invest in the coat's proper condition. You cannot feed an inexpensive supermarket brand and still think that your dog's coat is going to look like that Best

in Show Poodle at Madison Square Garden! Top show dogs, whose coats shimmer with quality, eat the best food.

Studies have proven that many of the cheaper dog foods do not supply the proper nutrients needed to support good health. Research also tells us that because of the poor nutritional quality in the less expensive foods, you have to feed larger quantities to maintain proper body weight. Top-quality dog foods provide a more digestible product that contains the proper balance of the vitamins, minerals and fatty acids that are necessary for healthy muscle, skin and coat. To reduce it to its simplest terms, dogs that eat cheap food "poop" more!

Don't be intimidated by all those dog-food bags on the store shelves. Read the labels and call the infor-

A pat for a polite Poodle! Well-behaved Poodles know that food and drink on the table is for their owners only—no begging allowed.

mation numbers on the dog-food bags. Ask your breeder and your vet what food they recommend for your pup. A solid education in canine nutrition will provide the tools you need to offer your his health. To keep your Poodle in prime condition, feed a quality food that is appropriate for his age and lifestyle. Premium manufacturers have developed their formulas with strict quality

Water must always be available for your Poodle, indoors and out, especially when exercising or in warm weather.

dog a diet that is best for his long-term health. Again, the quality of your dog's diet can determine the quality of controls, using only ingredients obtained from reliable sources. The labels on the food bags tell you what products are in the food and list ingredients in descending order of weight or amount in the food.

Dry food is recommended by most breeders and vets, since the dry particles help clean the dog's teeth of plaque and tartar. Adding water to dry food is optional. The food hog who almost inhales his food will do better with a splash of water in his food pan. A bit of water added immediately before eating is also thought to enhance the flavor of the food while still preserving the dental benefits. You can also add a couple of spoonfuls of a canned food to the dry kibble to add extra flavor for one meal a day. Whether feeding wet or dry, always have water available at all times.

Adult dogs will need to be fed twice per day, once in the morning and once in the evening. Some owners

BLOAT IN THE STANDARD POODLE

Deep-chested breeds are prone to the deadly condition known as bloat, caused by rapid accumulation of air in the subsequent rotation of the stomach. Further, studies suggest a genetic predisposition in the Standard Poodle, who is at high risk. Owners should take precautions to protect their dogs from the possible onset of bloat. Here are some commonsense steps to avoid your dog's swallowing air while he's eating or upsetting his digestion:

• Buy top-quality dog food that is high nutrition/low residue. Test the kibble in a glass of water. If it swells up to four times its original size, try another brand.

• No exercise one hour before and after all meals.

• Never allow your dog to gulp his food or water. Feed him when he is calm.

• Add small amounts of canned food to the dry.

Discuss further preventatives and the symptoms with your vet, as immediate treatment is necessary to save an affected dog's life.

CHAPTER 11

prefer to feed once per day, but this is the less effective way of feeding dogs and not as good for a dog's digestion. Scheduled feedings are always preferable to free-feeding, that is, leaving a bowl of food out all day so the dog can eat whenever he wants. Free-feeding dogs tend to become picky eaters, and it is more difficult to evaluate how much the dog is eating daily, especially when using a large feeder device or when there are multiple dogs in the household.

Like people, dogs have different appetites; some will lick their food bowls clean and beg for more, while others pick at their food and leave some of it untouched. It's easy to overfeed the chow hound! The author's basic rule (for dogs and people) is: lean is healthy, fat is not. Under-

Underneath that abundant coat should be a trim, muscular body, kept in top condition through proper diet and exercise.

Dry food is helpful in keeping plaque away, as are chew toys with dental benefits. Safe rope toys are one example; they act in a similar way to dental floss as the dog chews.

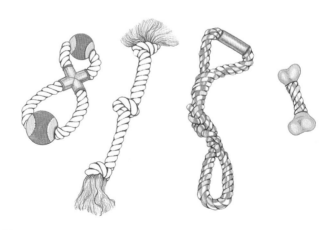

neath your Poodle's coat should lie a lean, muscular dog, capable of swimming, running and playing. Overweight dogs don't have energy and quickly become "couch Poodles." Research has proven that obesity is a major canine killer. Quite simply, a lean dog lives longer than one who is overweight. And that doesn't even reflect the better quality of life for the lean dog that can run, jump and play without the burden of extra poundage.

A coat like this doesn't "just happen." A full, healthy Poodle coat is a product of good health, good grooming, good breeding and good feeding.

FEEDING YOUR POODLE

Overview

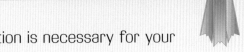

- Quality dog food with complete nutrition is necessary for your Poodle to stay in optimal condition of body, mind and coat.
- Take your breeder's advice as to what to feed your puppy and how to change your Poodle's diet as he grows up, including age at which to switch, amounts to feed and feeding schedule.
- Fresh drinking water is an essential component of any dog's diet.
- A feeding routine based on scheduled mealtimes is a better way to feed your Poodle than free-feeding.

Grooming Your Poodle

Intelligent, versatile and stylish, the Poodle is all of these and more in a stunning package. Regarded as the most magnificent coat in the dog world, the Poodle's coat places certain demands on his adoring owners. Even if you do not like the sculptured appearance of a fully groomed show Poodle, you will still have to tend to your dog's coat and have it trimmed in one manner or another. You don't want to see your adult Poodle without a haircut! You will be living with a matted bush on four legs! The coat

Poodles and their owners can look forward to spending lots of grooming time together, so it's best to get the pup used to it at a young age. A soft wire slicker brush can be used to gently brush through the puppy coat.

grows and grows and grows! Whether you have a Standard, Miniature or Toy, you have a heavily coated breed that will require grooming at least weekly at home as well as bi-monthly visits to a professional groomer.

Essential grooming equipment includes a grooming table for your dog to lie on, a pin brush, a small slicker brush, a wide-toothed metal comb, a fine metal comb and clippers. Your local pet store should be able to find the appropriate equipment for you. You may find a spray bottle handy for applying a light mist of water or some grooming conditioner. You will also need a pair of scissors for neatening up the feet and the tail.

Your breeder should be able to give you a basic lesson in grooming the Poodle. Your Poodle should be brushed out every week to keep the coat from matting. Lay the dog down and, starting from the center of the

All soaped up! Too-frequent bathing is never advised; how frequently you bathe will be decided by when the dog needs it and possibly also the show schedule if yours is a show dog.

The mature Poodle coat requires more grooming than that of a puppy, and regular brushing is the basis of a mat-free coat. Be sure to pay attention to the whole body, being extra-careful in the harder-to-reach sensitive areas.

back up near the ears, brush a small amount of coat toward the table and continue this until you have groomed down to the stomach. Turn him over and groom the other side.

Bathe your Poodle only as needed, as frequent bathing will remove the oil from the coat. If you plan to show your Poodle, your breeder or the local Poodle club will have to assist you in show grooming. Show grooming, done well, is an art and a skill and cannot be learned in a short period of time.

There are various pet trims for the Poodle. The breed standard lists the three acceptable clips for the show ring as the puppy clip (for young dogs only), the English saddle pattern and the Continental clip. However, almost any kind of trim in which the dog looks like a Poodle is acceptable for your pet. If you do not want to trim your dog yourself, your local pet grooming shop should be able

to do an excellent clip for your dog. However, it is still very important that you keep his coat brushed out weekly. Your groomer can trim your dog every two to three months and you will have a smart Poodle at your side.

POODLE PEDICURE

It is important to trim your dog's toenails, and it is best to start this within a week of bringing him home. Purchase a quality toenail trimmer for pets. Your first aid kit contains styptic powder in case you trim the nail too short and bleeding starts. If your dog's toenails are light in color, you will easily see the blood vessel that runs inside the nail. However, it is a bit more difficult to see it in dark-toed dogs, and you may nick the blood vessel until you are more familiar with trimming the nails. If you do not start trimming the nails at a young age, so your dog is used to this, you will have greater difficulty in trimming the nails as the dog becomes larger, heavier and more difficult to hold. If you have your dog groomed on a regular basis, the groomer will also trim his toenails.

FROM TOP TO BOTTOM

When your dog is a young pup you should start getting him used to an examination routine during grooming. Each time he is groomed, you should check over his ears, eyes, teeth and anal sacs.

Ears should be checked for dirt or any sign of infection. Take a damp cloth (a soft old washcloth can work quite well) and clean the inside of the ear while gently pulling out the long hairs in the ear. If you notice any build-up of wax, or a putrid smell, you should take your dog to the veterinarian to have the ears properly cleaned. If there is an infection, the vet will prescribe an ointment or liquid to clear up the problem. Dogs with upright ears have more of a chance of dirt getting into the ears, whereas dogs with

drop ears like Poodles have a "warm" ear where infections can grow more easily. If you see your dog shaking his head from side to side, or pushing his head and ear along the side of the furniture or carpet, you can be

After a bath, your Poodle should be dried thoroughly with a dryer on low heat, placed at a comfortable distance from the dog. To ensure a handsome, tangle-free result, you must brush as you dry.

almost certain that an ear infection is in the making.

When grooming, take a damp washcloth and gently clean the eyes and the surrounding areas. Light-colored Poodles may have visible tear stains, for which a suitable cleanser is available.

All dogs should have their eyes checked if any redness appears. Quite often you can purchase an over-the-counter medication at the pet shop and clear up the redness. If an eye problem persists, you will have to see your veterinarian.

Teeth should also be checked on a regular basis. You can clean your dog's teeth yourself by using a washcloth or a piece of gauze wrapped around your finger. Gently rub

Poodle owners should learn how to properly use electric clippers, as many of the various Poodle "haircuts" involve areas that are clipped.

your finger back and forth across the teeth as you would a toothbrush. Do not use human toothpaste, but you will find "doggy" toothpaste available if you wish to use it. If you allow plaque to build up, your dog will have as many dental problems as you would have.

Veterinarians will clean your dog's teeth, but it is a costly process and does not need to be done by a professional if you have done your work. Giving your dog several dog biscuits a day, plus his dry kibble, will help prevent the buildup of plaque.

As a dog ages, as in humans, his gums may recede and he will have further problems along with very smelly breath. Your vet may tell you that it is necessary to remove one or more teeth, but most dogs continue to eat well even if all of their teeth have been pulled. Of course, their diet will be a bit different, but they will fare just as well. A distinct, unpleasant odor from the mouth is a signal that all is not well with your dog's gums or teeth.

All dogs have anal sacs located on either side of the rectum. The contents, very smelly, are used to mark the dog's territory and are usually released when the dog defecates. Occasionally these will have to be expressed by hand. Have your veterinarian show you how to do this the first time and then you can do it at home, even though it is a rather smelly and unpleasant job! A sign that the anal glands are clogged is when your dog will scoot across the floor on his fanny. On occasion, the glands will appear swollen, which can be seen on a smooth-coated dog. Impacted anal glands will require veterinary attention.

The eyes, ears, teeth and anal glands are part of the general housekeeping of a dog.

Start your dog on this overall care routine at a very early age, doing a bit at a time, and, when your dog is an adult, you will have little difficulty in performing these cleaning functions.

Give your Poodle a weekly brushing, keep his toenails trimmed and his eyes, ears and teeth clean, take him to the groomer every couple of months and you will have a magnificently coated dog that looks and smells good and is a pleasure to have as a companion.

GROOMING YOUR POODLE

Overview

- With the most magnificently coated breed in dogdom, you can bet that grooming is a huge and important part of life with your Poodle.
- Poodle grooming usually requires the assistance of a professional groomer to keep him in a proper pet or show trim.
- Aside from trips to the groomer, the Poodle requires at least a thorough weekly brushing at home.
- Grooming also includes clipping the nails and tending to the dog's eyes, ears, teeth and anal sacs.

Keeping the Poodle Active

With a breed as bright and on-the-go as the Poodle, an active lifestyle makes for the happiest Poodle and the most sane owner. Poodle owners and their Renaissance dogs are looking for something challenging. Fortunately, today there are many activities to keep both of you busy, active and interested. Poodles can excel in any number of activities because of their intelligence, athleticism, willingness to please and adaptability. After Puppy Kindergarten, you may want to work toward the AKC's

Your Poodle is a sturdy and energetic dog that will continue to amaze you with his athletic feats.

Canine Good Citizen® Award. This program, when successfully completed, shows that your dog will mind his manners at home, in public places and with other dogs. This class is available to dogs (pure-bred or otherwise) of any age. It's a fun course and useful for everyday life. There are ten steps, including accepting a friendly stranger, sitting politely for petting, accepting light grooming and examination from a stranger, walking on a loose lead, coming when called, responding calmly to another dog, responding to distractions, down on command and remaining calm when the owner is out of sight for three minutes. Upon successful completion, your dog will receive an AKC Canine Good Citizen® certificate.

Going back to his water-dog origins, your Poodle will enjoy a day splashing in the surf or playing retrieving games on the beach with you.

With the young pup, you will find that he likes to play games with his safe toys, which include durable chews and knotted rope toys.

Games of fetch with his favorite person will keep the Poodle happily occupied.

There are some precautions that owners can take to protect their Poodles' coats when active and/or outdoors, such as fastening the headfall and ear feathering back with elastics.

All puppies like to chase a ball and return it to their owners, but be sure that the size of the ball (or any toy) is appropriate to the size of the Poodle—too large will be useless and too small can be dangerous.

Obedience is a sport at which all sizes of Poodle can excel. Obedience trials are held either by themselves or in conjunction with an AKC dog show. There are many levels, starting with Novice, whereupon completion of three passing "legs," the dog will earn a Companion Dog (CD) title. The courses then continue in difficulty, with Open at the second level; the dog earns a Companion Dog Excellent (CDX) upon completion of three successful legs. The next level is Utility (UD), which includes off-lead work, silent hand signals and picking the right dumbbells from a group of dumbbells. Not many dogs reach this level, and it is a major accomplishment for both owner and dog when a Utility degree is achieved.

Quick in mind and body, the Poodle is a natural success in agility competition. This illustration depicts the dog walk, testing the dog's balance and accuracy.

Agility trials have become all the rage in America and can be easily found at dog shows. Look for the large, noisy ring filled with competitors and dogs running the course and excited spectators watching at ringside, joining in with cheers. Some agility trials are held by themselves, not

A good way to exercise your Poodle is...another Poodle! Dogs enjoy the company of canine playmates and will motivate each other to stay active.

in conjunction with a conformation show.

Dogs are taught to run a course that includes hurdles, ladders, jumps and a variety of other challenges. There are a number of degrees in agility depending upon the obstacles that the dog is able

to conquer. AKC defines the goals of this sport as "The enjoyment of bringing together communication, training, timing, accuracy and just plain fun in the ultimate game for you and your dog." It also means lots of exercise for both dog and owner.

The ultimate in degrees is the Versatile Companion Dog, a title that well befits the Poodle! This is the degree that recognizes those dogs and handlers who have been successful in multiple dog sports.

In order to excel at any of the aforementioned activities, it is essential to belong to a dog club where there are equipment and facilities for practice. Find a good school in your area and attend a class as a spectator before enrolling. If you like the facility, the instructor and the type of instruction, sign your dog up for the next series of lessons, which will probably be two times a week with a choice of mornings or evenings.

These sports have become so popular with the public that there should be little difficulty in finding a training facility. If you belong to a Poodle club, other club members can help you get involved. You will find it a great experience to work with your dog and meet new people with whom you will have a common interest. This will all take time and interest on your part, and a willing dog working on the other end of the leash.

Of course, the easiest way to keep your dog active and fit is to take him for a walk every morning and evening. This will also be good for you! Playing games with your dog will delight him. You will find that your versatile Poodle is well suited to many activities and loves to be with you, so he can accompany you in many of the things that you do. All of these things done together will nuture a wonderful dog/owner bond.

KEEPING THE POODLE ACTIVE

Overview

- There's not much an owner can't do with his energetic and intelligent Poodle.
- An area of interest for many Poodle fanciers is conformation showing, as Poodles are natural showmen, attracting much attention in the ring.
- Poodles of all varieties fare well in obedience and agility competition, with obstacles being adjusted in size according to the size of the dogs.
- Your Poodle will love to participate in anything he can do with you. Participate in a training class together or just spend time playing and keeping active in pursuits that the two of you can share.

Your Poodle's Pal: The Vet

Before bringing your Poodle puppy home, you will need to find a good veterinarian. Your breeder, if from your area, should be able to recommend someone. Otherwise, it will be your job to find a clinic that you like.

When looking for a veterinarian, you will want to find someone, for convenience, who is within ten miles of your home. Find a veterinarian that you like and trust. You have to be confident that he knows what he is doing, as it is your dog's life at stake! Dogs have died for no good reason because a vet

Your vet will manage all aspects of your Poodle's vaccination schedule, from his puppy inoculation program to his adult booster shots.

didn't recognize a breed-specific problem. One case in point that is most obvious to Poodle owners and hopefully to their vets is hypoglycemia in Toy Poodles. Low blood sugar can incapacitate a 1-pound Toy, who will swiftly recover if offered a teaspoon of honey or carob syrup. Make sure your vet knows Poodles and likes them!

You love your Poodle and always want him to stay smiling and healthy, so you'll be sure to provide him with the best in medical care.

See that the vet's office looks and smells clean. It is your right to check on fees before setting up an appointment, and you will usually need an appointment. If you have a satisfactory visit, take the business card so that you have the clinic's number and the name of the veterinarian that you saw. Try and see the same vet at each visit, as he will personally know the history of your dog and your dog will be familiar with him.

Inquire if the clinic takes emergency calls and, if they do not,

Poodles are hardy dogs that can adapt well to changes in their condition. This ten-year-old is blind, but still looking alert and sprightly.

as many no longer do, get the name, address and telephone number of the emergency veterinary service in your area and keep this with your veterinarian's phone number. Check out the emergency clinic, too, before you actually need to use their services. Hopefully, you never will.

On your first visit, take along the records that your breeder gave you with details of the shots that your puppy has had so that the veterinarian will know which series of shots your pup should be getting. You should also take in a fecal sample for a worm test.

The recommended vaccines are for distemper, infectious canine hepatitis, parvovirus infection and parainfluenza. Although this seems like a lot of shots to give a dog, there is one shot that will cover all of these viruses: DHLPP. This series of shots will start between six and ten weeks, which means that the breeder will be giving the first

shots to his litter and the vet will have to finish up the series of three shots, given at four-week intervals.

Here's a basic explanation of the diseases for which vets inoculate:

- Distemper at one time was the scourge of dog breeding, but with the proper immunization and a clean puppy rearing area, this no longer presents a problem to the reputable breeder;
- Canine hepatitis, very rare in the United States, is a severe liver infection caused by a virus;
- Leptospirosis is an uncommon disease that affects the kidneys; it is rare in young puppies, occurring primarily in adult dogs;
- Parvovirus is recognized by fever, vomiting and diarrhea. This is a deadly disease for pups and can spread very easily through their feces. The vaccine is highly effective in prevention.

Poodles can be affected by

certain health problems of which a puppy buyer should be aware. Some of these are genetic problems and can be detected by tests. You should ask your breeder if any of

(PRA), which refers to diseases that affect the retina of the eye. If the problem is overlooked, blindness will eventually occur. This is an inherited disease and there are several different

At your Poodle's regular visits, your vet will give him a thorough hands-on examination to check for lumps, bumps or other abnormalities not obvious to the eye.

these problems are in his line and if he has had the sire and dam of the litter tested for and cleared as free of the problems. All three sizes of the Poodle have problems that relate to the eyes, skin and ears.

Eye problems include progressive retinal atrophy

types of the disease. Yearly eye examinations by a veterinary ophthalmologist are recommended for all Poodles.

Sebaceous adenitis, a gland inflammation, is a serious problem, especially in the Standard Poodle. This is thought to be a genetic disease and the Poodle Club of

America is working diligently to rid the breed of this problem by asking that all breeding dogs be tested for the disease with a skin biopsy. Clinical signs are diminishing coat quality, scaling and hair loss. This is a discouraging disease for the owner, as it is hard to cure. The main treatment is antiseborrheic shampoos and other experimental therapies.

Hip dysplasia is a major concern, as it is in most medium-sized and large breeds. Hip dysplasia is an inherited disease in which the head of the femur (thigh bone) fails to fit into the socket in the hip bone and there is not enough muscle mass to hold the joint together. This can often be a very painful problem for the dog, causing him to limp or to move about with great difficulty. There are various types of surgical and therapeutic treatment options, depending on the severity of the dysplasia. All Standard and Miniature Poodles that are bred should have normal hips as determined by an x-ray and

A telltale sign of aging is lightening hair on the muzzle, much like graying in humans. A puppy playmate can help get a senior up and moving, but be aware of the extra attention that the older dog will need.

approved by the Orthopedic Foundation for Animals (OFA).

Von Willebrand's disease is a blood clotting disease similar to hemophilia, but in dogs it will affect both sexes. If an affected dog has the disease and is injured or has surgery, he may bleed more than a dog without the disease. If the disease is severe, there may be spontaneous bleeding from the nose, mouth or bladder. Dogs are tested by a blood sample and dogs with VWD should not be bred, as it is a hereditary disease.

Hypothyroidism, the most common of hormonal disorders in dogs, can be found in the Standard Poodle. Hypothyroidism is a deficiency of the thyroid hormone. Signs of this disease can be lethargy, exercise intolerance, weight gain and changes in the coat. This can be treated with a synthetic thyroid hormone given on a daily basis.

Other problems, on a lesser basis, are Addison's

Your vet will take your Poodle's temperature and record all of his vital signs. You should do this at home as well so that you have normal figures against which to compare if ever you suspect that your Poodle is under the weather.

disease, Cushing's disease, epilepsy and Legg-Calve-Perthes disease. Many of these diseases can be tested for in breeding animals, and you should check with your breeder and see the test results for the sire and dam of your puppy's litter.

Ask to see the certificates with the appropriate registries and do not just accept his word that the sire and dam of the litter have been tested for the various problems. This list may seem daunting, but responsible breeders will have had their stock tested and will be doing their best to eliminate these problems in the breed by excluding any affected dogs from breeding programs. For further information on any of the aforementioned health issues, check out the Poodle Club of America's website.

Toothbrushes and specially formulated doggy toothpaste are available to help owners care for their dogs' dental health, an important component of his overall well-being.

Health guarantees are important, and a responsible breeder will give you a contract that guarantees your pup against certain congenital defects. This guarantee will be limited in time, probably to six months or one year. If there is a problem, the breeder should be willing to possibly replace the pup or offer some refund in his price. Hopefully you will get a healthy pup right off the bat and develop a good rapport with a knowledgeable vet who has experience with the Poodle and knows how to keep him in top condition.

YOUR POODLE'S PAL: THE VET

Overview

- You must find a skilled vet whom you trust, one located conveniently and who has sufficient knowledge of the Poodle and its breed-specific health issues.
- Your vet will give your pup an overall exam and pick up with his vaccinations where the breeder left off.
- Poodles begin life with the healthiest start when bred from parents who have been tested for and certified as clear of genetic diseases.
- Acquaint yourself with the problems to which the Poodle can be prone so that you are better prepared to give your dog the best care.